Not So Long Ago

Marc Gregory: Collected Lyrics
1976–2019

nprnt press

First printing: October 2015
Second printing: March 2020

published by
nprnt press
www.nprntpress.com

ISBN 978-1-9992812-1-2

"And in between what might have been and what has come to pass, a misbegotten guess, alas, and bits of broken glass..."

—James Taylor

Contents

i   PREFACE

Part One: *Love Songs (more or less...)*

1   Alone

3   Running and Hiding

6   Holly

9   Love's Gone

11   One for Always

13   Somebody Said...

15   Halfway in the Air

17   Another Day, Another Year

20   Fine Time

23   The Thing About It Is

26   About to Break

28   Can't Say Why

30   Now and Then (The Barter)

33   One Up (on the Other)

35   Tough Dice

37   Your Guess Is As Good As Mine

39   Doesn't Seem So Very Long Ago

41   But One Thing

44   Chelsea Girl

47   Love in the Mainstream

50   Quite Unchanged

52   Quiet Serenade

Part Two: *Other Things (in a time of stress...)*

56   Some People

58   Late Night Lullaby

60   Bottom Line

63   Mind Is Gone

65   Got To Have It

69   Any Way You Want Me

72   The Good Witch of the East

75   What the Heart and Mind Decide

77   Showers

79   Song for a Young Girl

82   Life on the Line

85   Midwinter Down

87   Beat to the Wide

90   Not Again

92   The Grifter

94   Anything You Say

97   Numbers

100   Echoes of Atrocities Past

102   Now's the Time

105   What's It Gonna Be Today?

108   But They Were Mine

111   The Greatest Country in the World

115   Never

117   Not So Long Ago

120   Always At a Certain Time of Day

123   Early Fallen for Summer

125   Calendar of Moons

128   Look Ahead

131   Nothing Left to Say

PREFACE

Writing lyrics for popular songs is a tricky proposition.
Inevitably, one will confront the issue of trying to find
new and different ways of saying things that have
already been said a thousand times before. This is
especially true in trying to write what seems to be,
for better and for worse, the core currency of the
whole practice— "love" songs. Whatever the kind of
song, songwriting is an effort in trying to make use of
a set of experiences and a common cultural language
in a way that will resonate with people. So it is with
the songs in this volume.

Except for a few forays, I didn't even try to write
lyrics until I was in my 30s. Familiar as I was with the
work of Paul Simon, Joni Mitchell, Jackson Browne,
Gordon Lightfoot, James Taylor and many others, I
felt more than a little daunted. Not to mention John
Lennon. Not to mention Stephen Sondheim, and not
to mention stand-out lyricists of earlier eras, like
Ira Gershwin, Lorenz Hart, Cole Porter and Johnny
Mercer, again among others.

My orientation was always more towards music and, with respect to words, thought "Well, I'm never going to be that good, so why bother?" But one often feels compelled to say things one really wants to say. So those mentioned above are a bit like stars to aim for. If those heights are not quite attainable, one is perhaps able, in making the effort, to draw out one's best. Consequently, after having thrown out some early efforts that struck me as weak or substandard, I set out, rather humbly, to say what it was I wanted to say.

Which brings us to the work set forth in this collection. Most of the time, people who write songs are trying to SAY SOMETHING. They are trying to comment upon, or put into a certain perspective, an issue they consider relevant or important. At other times, they're simply offering a take on the vagaries of life, or even just looking to write some likeable song that might be appealing—but hopefully without being idiotic and lame. At present, as in the past, there is no shortage of popular tunes that are lame beyond description; trivial in conception and inept in execution. But with a legitimate and sincere sense of purpose, some talent and a little luck, one can avoid creating a whole lot of drivel. (Then again, one person's drivel is another's poetry. So it goes.)

Dispensing, hopefully, with absolute drivel, there are examples of different kinds of songs here. It will be apparent to the reader which is which, and this underscores the obvious: songwriters, like everyone else, respond in their way to all of life's situations, challenges, ups, downs, joys and sorrows.

Structurally, many of the lyrics here conform to a verse/verse/chorus/bridge framework, while others exhibit different or more ambitious forms. In some cases, characters I have contrived do the speaking in the songs. As if in a Broadway musical, they stand at the center of these little fictions and one looks through their eyes and speaks as they might. It affords a writer some distance, allowing him/her to function more as an observer. It also allows the writer to obliquely comment, now and then, on things tangential to the narrative of the song. In other cases, the expression is pretty direct. But it is a fallacy to assume that every word a writer writes is a direct expression of who they are. Songwriters like to tell stories, some more personal, some less so.

Readers may notice that on a very few occasions I have borrowed a bit of a phrase here and there. This is done consciously and deliberately. Nothing is ever created in a vacuum, and the extent to which we are excessively and almost neurotically proprietary about a line or a brief series of notes has a great deal to do with the amount of money that circulates in music publishing. This is in no way to be construed as a justification for borrowing a little too freely. But we have a rather constricted view of what "originality" means, a view that would have been considered confining and excessively severe in other eras.

As a writer of my time, of a generation now stretching the boundaries of middle age, the work here partakes of the ethos of a certain era, while at the same time seeking to transcend the confines of that, or any era. Having travelled some and lived abroad, I am also something of a writer of place as well. That place would be L.A. It is the city in which I was born and raised, and many of my formative experiences occurred there. It is a city that has bred or attracted to it many legendary songwriters whom I greatly admire. And, it is a city that has exerted a huge influence on popular culture in general. Creative people are in large part formed by the soil in which they first grew, and the residue of that environment often stays with them forever.

Popular songs are a huge part of the cultural currency of our time. In some instances, they help characterise and render indelible our experiences, from the most sober and profound to the most light-hearted and whimsical. Songs accompany people throughout their lives as good friends of a sort, friends we are often happy to hear from or turn to. And so, in scope, they encompass almost everything that comes our way. It is with this in mind that one tries, to the best of one's ability, to participate in the kind of universal communication good songs make possible.

A certain debt of gratitude is owed to all the people (except one or two) with whom I crossed paths and who prompted the writing of these songs. I would also like to express a very special and sincere thank you to my dear friends Raymond Shaw, himself a fine poet and painter, and Jessica Webster, a gifted and lovely person, for making it possible for me to publish this book. Thanks are due as well to my friend Meryl Tihanyi for her visual acumen, her cover photograph and her help with graphic design and layout of the cover.

There is a difference between being serious, which I am, and self-serious, which I am not. If the words in this book strike a few resonant chords and also give rise to a smile or two, I will be more than content. If not...well, thanks anyway. Apart from that, there is nothing left to say.

Marc Gregory
Berkeley, California
December 2019

PART ONE

Love Songs (more or less...)

Alone

Why am I alone right now?
Here I lie, just feeling sorry for myself
You have come and gone
But traces linger on
Traces of things we used to know

Maybe you're alone right now
And do you still feel something
For me within yourself?
Think about trying again
But then, why pretend?
Nothing's different now, but for this new indifference

You told me I'd reach for you
You wouldn't be around
There in the distant breaking light
Nothing, not a sound
Pride is such a hollow feeling
As it conquers and divides
It's all you really need to cover
The hollow you feel inside

So we're both alone right now
There's no doubt—
Just take a look around
Another pair come and gone
But one trace lingers on
The one of this new indifference

1976

Running and Hiding

You say you're gonna miss me
And I wonder if that's true
The vengeful back-talk
How did we survive?
And now you blow-the-kiss me
Beg me not to misconstrue
The contrasting residue
Tepid grey and washed-out hue

It got a little hazardous
To look into your eyes
Was there something there
I never knew?
All the shadowed secrets
And the oft-contested lies
The fits and starts and tries
The unconfirmed goodbyes

You're running and hiding at the right time
Looking to make the next deal
Taking the head start I'd given you
And looking for more you can steal

You love the scent of danger
Only if it's just so strong
Plot another innocent's demise
A secondary stranger
To hold you just so long
Make you feel like you belong
And just as he's there, you're gone

Another summer movie
Which you take in novelised
Another game of catch-me-if-you-can
In every getaway scene that
You have memorised
The sap characterised
The plot unrealised

You're shucking and jiving all the right lines
Yet it all seems so surreal
Love's not the contest you've made of it
A shell-game with nothing revealed

You could have just told me
That's how it is
That things could just go so far
Instead you short-sold me
To trade thick for thin
But that's just the way that you are

So keep the faded flowers
Of your second-hand regard
Scorch the future with your need to win
I'll try to replace the hours
Exploited and off-guard
Misspent and par hasard
Never to be redeemed again

You're running and hiding at the right time
But it all seems so unreal
Shortchanging answers for alibis
Sticking pins for others to feel

2004

Holly

Bright red hair
Or so it seemed
A single bag was packed
To head out of Tennessee

First up north
Then out west
Better lean on what she tells you, boy
'Cos you might never know the rest

Ooh Holly
Won't you settle down baby?
And quit acting like you never knew
Oh Holly,
I don't think I mean maybe
'Cos I think I got plans for you
Ooh Holly
Won't you settle down baby?
And quit acting like you never knew

I always see you passing
So many days gone by
Sometimes I think of asking
But I can't remember why

But you know what I'm thinking
More than I can say
And you raise so many questions
That needed answers anyway

And damned if you don't belong there
Up where you want to be
In between the passing stages
And in between men like me

I know you're always searching
Does it matter anymore?
When the search becomes the reason
You don't find what you're looking for

You might find
You made it OK
When you look back and realise
That it really didn't matter anyway

'Cos you went your way
And I went mine
Kind of worked out like it was supposed to
'Cos we was only passing time

Ooh Holly
Won't you settle down baby?
And quit acting like you never knew
Oh Holly
Guess I have to say maybe
'Cos I thought I had plans for you
Ooh Holly
Won't you settle down baby?
And quit acting like you never knew

Ooh Holly
Won't you settle down baby?
And quit acting like you never knew
Oh Holly
Guess I have to say maybe
'Cos I thought you had plans for me too
Ooh Holly
Won't you settle down baby?
And quit acting like you never knew...
Never knew

1986

Love's Gone

Sometimes you never know when you might find her
And even if you do, she could slip away
All that you can hope is to remind her
You love her in no ordinary way

Done what you can, you wonder if she'll catch on
Till it colors every move you make
With every regret you think you set too much on
Every promise she decides to break

Why —why does it always come down to this?
I —look so casual while I'm floating signs of distress

And she said
Love knows where you're going
Who knows where you've been
But something is showing
Of the pointless, half-run races
With unremembered faces
Scattered traces of all the in-betweens

Men are so vain and clumsy
It's very plain to see
Mostly just sad and lonely
And no exception is me
No, no exception is me...

It goes how it goes you wonder just what went wrong
Taken in, you hit all the misses she gives
She still thinks it's time to keep the gloves on
You still think somehow you're going to win

Maybe you get to be a little frantic
As you try to comprehend her choice within
No need to ponder internal semantics
When the walls are crumbling and the roof is caving in

Why —when I'm just about buckling under the stress
Try —but you've made a fool of yourself for less

And she said
Love's gone and you know it
It's just that way
You and I both know
That with all the backwards glances
And endless second chances
There are no saving graces
In unremembered faces
And the scattered traces of all that might have been

1988 / 1994

One for Always*

My best friend says he needs a best man
Don't think I didn't have a clue
He keeps the promise of the very first day
When she ran his heart right through

The boy, he never was a mark so easy
Always found a way to have his way
The girl, she wasn't quite what he expected
She figured how to make him stay
Now he won't have it any other way

One for always
And one for now
And one for forever
So maybe that's how it begins

Can't stay together, so temperamental
That's what I hear so many others say
But this one's more than just sentimental
If some edges tatter, still they don't fray

For some, this kind of thing, it just ain't easy
With all the feign and shuck and endless jive
Others, through the years it stays light and breezy
Three homes, two kids, three sets of forks and knives
The one thing this one stays is alive

You get the funny feeling that they've been
here before
When you see the little sparkle in their eyes
You spend your time stealing through open doors
Just then you realise...

One for always
No need for concern
'Cos they've got each other
And lots of time to burn

One for always
No more to say
This one's for always
Maybe just forever and a day
And they won't have it any other way

1985

Written as a wedding present for some dear friends.

Somebody Said...

I know you've heard it all a thousand times before
I know you don't want to hear it anymore
I can't tell you how I feel
'Cos the words make it all
So unreal

But somebody said something about
You were thinking maybe leaving me behind
Can't get it out, out of my head
Another like you I could never hope to find

Seems like forever since we stepped into this dream
Wonder why never are things quite the way
they seem?
Time was never on our side
But you could have seen
How hard I tried

Say what you want
Say what you will
But don't say goodbye
Till we get a chance to feel...

How it would be if we could work this whole thing out
What we would be if we could move it past all doubt
I can't tell you how it'd feel
But it all could be
So unreal

But somebody said
Something about
You were thinking maybe leaving me behind
Can't get it out, out of my head
Another like you I could never hope to find

1987

Halfway in the Air

I saw it then when you walked out this morning
Stealing out the door, like every other time
Giving in again when it gets complicated
Giving up the search for what we still could find

The sky turns clear and cold, and very blue
Endings aren't supposed to look this way
In the cab, don't turn back, don't hesitate
Don't even part with just the time of day

Make your way to the moving hallway
The one that leaves you halfway in the air
Drag the suitcase, tag your name
If the crew looks just the same
Soon you'll tilt the seat, look out to see what's there

Because you
You have to have something wrong
You can't let yourself belong
For too long
It isn't safe that way

It seems
It takes more than luck to reach your dreams
And when they're never what they seemed
One more slipstream
They just fade away

Sometimes you have to cling to something
with meaning
In the face of situations that don't last too long
In a sea of circumstances that haven't any
Double-back for what you missed as you went along

So you get to the moving hallway
The one that leaves you halfway in the air
Shade the window on the plane
If the emptiness remains
Steal a look inside, is anybody there?

Because you
You have to have something wrong
So you don't have to belong
For too long
It isn't safe that way

And I
All I can do is try
Try not to say the last goodbye
As I
Watch you walk away

1986

Another Day, Another Year*

Let it go
Turn it loose
You can't fight it
So what's the use?

Another day
Another year
Another lifetime
Might make it clear

Just how much she meant to you
You can't bring yourself to say
Just how much you let her down
And how you let her slip away

The time goes by
The years recede
In the pensive still shudder
Of half-remembered dreams
Were they as they seemed?

In a passing off-chance
By far too discreet
A crest of time lingers
And wanders incomplete

Of all the times not to say
All the things you should have said
You should have known the words would come
To someone else instead

And oh, you really should have known better than to
let it end this way
All the things you could have known together don't
come 'round every day

Take your time
Make it slow
Don't worry about it
Someday she'll know

What was there is gone
What a price you pay
As you shuffle along
Through every shade of grey
Each new shade of grey

Hold her close, don't let her go
In your heart, if nowhere else
In spite of all the things you know
You didn't know yourself
You didn't trust yourself

So let it go
Turn away
You won't forget her
Try as you may
And try as you may
It didn't have to be this way

1988

Written for a musical theatre production that never got off the ground.

Fine Time

I wouldn't do that if I were you
So sure of what you think you see
Maybe a reason to say we're through
Relax dear, it's only me

There's a little time if you're stuck on the line
Move you past those lingering doubts
It's a fine time, if you're so inclined
Never know what we might find out

It's a cool night
It's alright
Reach out and take my hand
Think it's just right,
So sit tight
We'll turn on a dime once again

The time comes 'round, but there you go
Not sure if you want to believe
A face wan like on an old scarecrow
Wondering who's left to deceive

And though it's not for me to say
What you should think or do
You can have it your own way
'Cos angel, you usually do

It's a fine line
The between times
Never do let you be
But we'd be on time
If you don't decline
The best is yet to be

Say don't tell me maybe, darling
My love for you is here to stay
We shouldn't be making any big decisions
While you're still carrying on this way
This way
This way...

Remember the early 2000s, darling
Integrity was so passé
We had the chance to make it so much better
But then that dream just got pissed away
Away
Away...

So what is it you're hanging on to?
Playing so close to the vest
Looking for someone else to belong to
When you'd already found the best

This hesitation doesn't suit you
Somewhat unhealthy, they say it might be
No trick in finding a suitable companion,
In such charmingly flawed company

It's a cool night
It's alright
Reach out and take my hand
Think it's just right
So sit tight
We'll turn on a dime once again

It's a fine time
To find time
Don't fret the anomalies
If you don't mind
Being resigned
Just leave the rest to me

1989/2009

The Thing About It Is

She and I spoke candidly
How lightly certain subjects need be tread
And I mentioned, somewhat off-handedly
Some things are better left unsaid

She said she didn't see it that way
All the pieces didn't seem to fit
And I said I didn't mean it that way
The way she seemed to be taking it

So many times we go 'round in circles
Never seem to find the way out
Never getting near what we need most to say
Stumbling as we do in self-doubt

And the thing about it is
That sometimes it's hard to know
If what it isn't or it is
Is never quick to quite unfold

And the thing about it is
When it comes down to why and where
If you can't find where something lives
That something maybe isn't there

I didn't say another chance was deserved
You might be thinking something else might do
But I'll take this chance to be not-quite-so-reserved
Come right out and say
How much I miss you

Sometimes a man just needs a little time
A little time to sit and think things through
Before he's ready to lay it on the line
But it doesn't mean he'd rather
Be without you

And the meaning of it is
That sometimes things aren't plain
And though they're very much alive
It isn't easy to explain

That the thing about it is
What makes me whole is you
So there's nothing I can say
And there's nothing I can do

And so what I mean is this
That if you would only stay
Then you'd see just what I mean
And I wouldn't have to say

That the thing about it is
I've just run out of things to say
It doesn't come as a surprise
I don't talk much anyway...

1989

About to Break

All you ever said was what's the difference?
But what am I to make of things like this?
You drew me in to keep me at a distance
Then left me to figure it, hit or miss

I'd withstand each fleeting indiscretion
With everything, I tried to bring you back
Each deliberate misinterpretation
Only slipped us that much more off track

What you take
Is so much more than what you give
About to break
Isn't any way to live

Lamenting now your unfound reputation
The one that you sustain with every act
And all of your gross miscalculation
Storms and strains and rages to hold you back

With every broken promise I would search
For the underlying meaning of it all
I'd find self-absorption and not much more
My voice unheard, my back against the wall

Every time
I would be there for you
Being there
Was something more than you could do

And what you take
Is so much more than what you give
About to break
Isn't any way to live
About to break
Is really no way to live

All you ever said was what's the difference?
Leaving me to figure hit or miss
I put up with all your mock indifference
But how can I forgive mistakes like this?
How can I forgive mistakes like this?

1989

Can't Say Why

Can't find much
To say
Don't think it matters anyway
Just the same
It's very plain

It takes
So long
Sometimes things just go wrong
Easily
Too easily

Long summer days
Filter back through a lifting haze
Days gone by
All gone by

What lies ahead
Is what you make of it instead
How can I
Just say goodbye?

'Cos I never realised
How close we came
Distant, once interwoven lives
Like broken sunlight through a misting rain
Turn and fall away again

Still the same
Old song
These things you've known all along
But don't know why
Can't say why

Why did it take all of these years
For us to come to see
That the best part of all the things we were
Was the one made of you and me?

Long summer days
Filter back through a lifting haze
Days gone by
All gone by

What lies
Ahead
Is what we make of it instead
And still I
Can't say goodbye

1988

Now and Then (The Barter)

No matter now in taking time to try
to shut down the pain
No matter how hard you try,
the answer's still the same
There's never time enough, it seems,
when you need it most
Time to realise youthful dreams,
though you forever hold them close

We bargain and negotiate with good intentions
up our sleeve
And in the barter lament the loss of
each misspent reprieve
Not to believe in something better,
or to heed a distant call
Or forfeit the price of sacrifices so exceedingly small,
So exceedingly small

Sacrifices of fear, of loneliness, of things you can
never quite explain
In the hope of filling the emptiness that seems
always to remain
Off in the distant reaches,
like a mist in the back of our minds
Shrouding half-remembered visions of
another place and time

And what a shame it is
When we finally come to see
That all the best things came and went
While we settled so carelessly

From time to time the thought rises again
To return to fresher, simpler times that demand and
place no blame
You remember there's no going back,
though you always do
And remain in the crossfire of now and then,
Waiting on another sometime to see you through.

So you make room for forgiveness,
the kind that isn't true
And you tell yourself it's better than nothing,
as if anything will do
And in the time it takes to settle the debt,
and total up the cost
That fleeting image of something better
becomes ineffably lost

Lost in the distant reaches,
shrouded by the relentless passage of time
A muted flame that faintly expires in a forgotten
corner of mind

(And what a shame it is
When we finally come to see
That the best things all came and went
While we settled so carelessly
And learned to love second-best
So effortlessly)

1989

One Up (on the Other)

When I come to you, defeating myself
Not knowing where it will end
You say it's no good repeating yourself
You've got to learn how to bend
You say it won't last forever
But habits are hard to break
Over and over it's just one or the other
I don't know how much more I can take

One up on the other
You know it's going to break you in two
One up on the other
Then there'll be nothing you can do

You say I refuse to understand
The things you say you must go through
The more I give in, the more you demand,
Burning both ends of a candle or two
A phase, you say, it can't last forever
Bad habits are hard to break
You just replace one with another
Take a quick breather, if just for my sake

One up on the other
You know it's going to break you in two
One up on the other
Then there'll be nothing you can do

Plan my day neatly
Play my cards discreetly
Watch it all fall to rubble in your wake
Never thought I'd be at such a loss
To know what move to make

The right thing to say comes out at the wrong time,
And we go right to the wrong conclusion
Day after day, it seems such a long time
To drift in the same old confusion

One up on the other
In a bit it'll break you in two
One up on the other
Then there'll be nothing you can do

When I come to you defeating myself
Not knowing where it will end
You say it's no good repeating yourself
There's nothing left to defend

1983

Tough Dice

U said
That's all
As I
Recall

Now ur thinkin'
Maybe 2wice
Gamble hard?
Tough dice

Think ur bad
Not so
1 big
Ego

Said it 1nce
Say it 2wice
Gamble with me
Tough dice

Come on, sugar
That all u got to show?
Nothin' but noise again
Nothin' I wanna know

U said
That's all
Nice trip
Bad fall

'Cos this fire
Just turned to ice
Played ur hand
Tough dice

1989

Your Guess Is As Good As Mine

You always want it your way, never mine
And I can't believe the emptiness I'm feeling
The things you say and do don't coincide
And the breach between the two just
leaves me reeling

There's no way to peel back the years
When the simple things seem always to elude you
There I am again with the same old fears
Wondering if it's possible to move you

'Cos it's always the same old line
Re-arranged from time to time
And everything else remains undefined
If I press you for an answer
You say maybe there's none to find
Your guess is as good as mine

I still remember how you used to be
But now it seems I'm talking to a stranger
The love you once expressed so easily
Now seems so fragile and endangered

But it's always the same old line
Restated but unrefined

Like a dusty relic from another time
The same old words do not serve
When they've lost their meaning and shine
Same old verse, same old pantomime

Now I don't want to live without you
But it's too late don't you see
When I find myself starting to doubt you
And all the things you've meant to me

Somehow things don't ever stay the same
And faith in change becomes the only answer
The way I feel doesn't seem to have a name
A wandering tune, a worn-out, ragged dancer

Now you look helplessly at me
Your kind of freedom isn't free
And you're wondering how much there might
be left in me
So you press me for an answer
As if maybe there was one to find
Well your guess is as good as mine
Your guess is as good as mine

1991

Doesn't Seem So Very Long Ago

The last time I saw you
It was late November
Gliding through a path of autumn snow
Winding ridge behind
Like an ashen-embered fire
Doesn't seem so very long ago

I'm not sure I knew
Just what you were thinking
Your hair pushed back with the falling autumn sky
But it seemed to me I saw
Something in you conspire
With the new oncoming winter
Not sure I knew the reason why

And I try
But it doesn't seem to do me any good
Something dies
Looking through this bare-branched, frozen wood

There's a promise in the air
You almost see it in a bright October
In turning leaves, on heat-stilled afternoons
But fragile as it dies
Muffled in unbroken silence
Bleeds still through every season and falls through

Too many northeast snowbreaks have come and gone
Neither saying what they had to say
Too many ice-bound dreams that never saw the dawn
And weathered seasons washed away

But you can stay
There's time enough to know
Time enough to find out who we are
Don't waste away
The only chance we'll know
Did we get this close just to remain so far?

And I try
But does anything turn out as it should?
Somehow I
Have let myself be so misunderstood

The last time I saw you
It was late November
You were flying through newfallen autumn snow
Soft hills close behind
Like an ashen-embered fire
It doesn't seem so very long ago
And still I think about the things
I never got to know

1989

But One Thing

Like to side-step everything
Take a sunlit walk in a park
Never know what each day brings
What do you think the chances are

That some time spent on our own
Could have mended everything?
Not so easy all alone
Together there's so much we
Bring to each other and then...

I get caught up in a daydream
Relive the good things gone sour
Not so hard as it may seem
When the air's clear,
The light's good at any hour

But one thing
I know
That no-one fails all the time
And if I can't
Let go
It may just mean that I'm...

Trying to sort a few things through
Where the misunderstanding lies
Doing whatever I have to do

To sift through the angry lies
And the strangeness of this compromise

What would you say
Could we try it all again?
There's always a way
For the strongest trees to bend
A little time-worn, but then...

But one thing
I know
And I've known it for quite a long time
It's that what does-
n't show
Runs deeper than what does sometimes
And you might just say that I'm...

Tired of everything that I've been through
And of all the things I've seen
And of all the disappointments we knew
And of everything that came between us
More and more that I try to do
Less and less do I seem to get through

So we're pretty much the same
No matter how much time goes by
If I end up with the blame
There's still a lot that never met your eye

And if you ever just think back
Wonder how all this began
If you look hard, you will find
How much of you I am

1989

Chelsea Girl

I know you think you've been done wrong
Seen even the small hopes defeated
But I have been here all along
Ever since you first retreated

But who's to say and who's to know
Which way your heart might be beating?
You say I'm wrong, I don't think so
It's always me you'll be misreading
It's defeating

Chelsea girl
Well I know you're what I needed
Chelsea girl
Can it ever be the same?
It's a whole new world
And that's a point that needs conceding
Still you're so sure
You know just where to put the blame

Now every small thought turns around
How there was just something about you
Each ventured guess turns upside-down
In every way you find to doubt it

But if I answered every claim
To breach the depths of your misgivings
Would your response still be the same?
Would I still meet with your indifference?

'Cos I have got a thousand whys
Each a better one to want you
It's endless nights and long goodbyes
And chances missed that ever haunt you
Haunt you

I know
You know
We all know how it can be
But if you know
Say so
Don't just leave it all to me

Chelsea girl
Is the memory receding?
At every turn
I've tried hard to understand
You'll walk away
From a story that needs completing
And let it all
Slip right through your hands
An empty fist of windblown sand

I know you think you've been done wrong
But some assumptions are misleading
What will it take for you to know
That some mistakes don't need repeating?

1993

Love in the Mainstream

I get so sick of love songs
But I write them anyway
As if to wrest new meaning
From the same worn-out clichés

Maybe in the mainstream
You can do it after all
Get past the empty maybes
The bright starts that stop and stall

She came from a good family
No-one ever gone astray
A negotiating factor
She kept firmly in your way

And then there were the good friends
Who had to have their say
You know of course she let them
She makes up her mind that way

Love in the mainstream
Middle-class to be quite sure
Love in the mainstream
Demographically secure

Inspected like a patent
Beyond a shadow of a doubt

Not even God can help you boy
The moment she finds out

You're something short of perfect
Prone to a mistake or two
Then she sets the agenda
And you're a house guest passing through
So there ain't much you can do

And as you turn your back on the last of fond hopes
Reluctant to be freed
You're turned 'round by the thought of all the things
She never could concede
Like the unmistakable greed
That's born to a certain breed

Love in the mainstream
Over-rated, if demure
Like love in the eighties
Upwardly mobile, as it were

Love in the mainstream
Understated, or just inferred
Like love on the flat screen
One small footfall past absurd

Maybe in the mainstream
You could do it after all

Pass on the empty maybes
The bright starts that stop and stall

But some myths are self-creating
And this may have been the case
A lie about the future's one
We all like to embrace

Life in the mainstream
Middle class to be quite sure
Love as a plain dream
Demographically secure

Love in the mainstream
A big sensation, if not quite pure
Life in the mainstream
And the time she took to make sure she's not sure

1990/2003

Quite Unchanged

I will survive
This roller-coaster ride with you
Though nothing I can do
Will make you see

It just takes time
And there is nothing I can say
Nothing you'll hear anyway
Nothing that will change your mind

In my way
Negotiated borderlines
Scattered hope that once was mine
But now slips away

It's easy to be right
Easy to place the blame
On everyone but yourself
Not to see that we're the same
Like two solitary shadows none will claim

Now I
Wouldn't say
You should try to see it my way
So far that's been too far for you to go
But you might
Anyway

As we get lost on the same old byways
Forever turning up the dust
On both shoulders of the road

And so I
Have just one thing to say to you
That will never not be true
However far you go

That through
All that we go through
Doing what we have to do
Down lonely or crowded avenues

And through
All its small and big mistakes
Or how many beats it takes
Or how fragile as it breaks
This heart will remain
Will remain
Just the same
Quite unchanged

1989

Quiet Serenade*

As we come to the end of this passion play
I don't think I can find anything left to say
Quite certain there is no more to be said
Any more certain and I might well be dead
Who knows, since last count I might be anyway
Since I'm so certain there isn't anything left to say

There's far too high a price to pay
To busk for love in this gallery
For light-hearted saints of this latter day
Whose dance on a ledge no longer plays
Who scans for a horizon that never will stray
Not now, nor someday
Far too high a price for me

How we get to where we are
Is still a complicated intrigue
Where good young men and ladies fair
Counting so many pasts in the folds of their sleeves
Like barques confronting mountainous waves
Are swallowed by such storming seas
Broken and cast upon distant shores
Spent in scattered, fragmented debris

These were folksongs of various kinds
As fortune inclines that they might be
Memories of what we leave behind

As they turn and fade in varied rhyme
Like lives falling in and out of time
Always seem to get the best of me
Glimpses of what was, what might have been
And perhaps of what is yet to be

So should you wonder how this came to pass
Or if it matters anyway
Perhaps you will see of yourself at last
Something in these songs
Or is it only me?

1990

Originally the last song of a cycle, intended to tie it all together.

PART TWO

Other Things *(in a time of stress...)*

Some People

Some people always seem to have it movin'
Got their cake and they eatin' on it too
All the time you're grindin', they'll be groovin'
Sayin' there's more for me when we leave
a little less for you

This routine maybe strike you as familiar
Like a scene from some bad movie seen long before
And each re-run's just that much more peculiar
Why bother getting up if only to fall once more?

But this person ain't gonna show you no jive intentions
Ain't gonna sell you no second rate point of view
I been through it all more times
than I care to mention
More times than I ever thought
I could see myself through

You know it's true, You know it's true
It's not about the things we say
It's about the things we do

Time and time again you see it happen
And you can't believe the noise
that people make is true

Never satisfied, they always reachin' and grabbin'
Gonna make you see it their way 'fore you're through

But now you look to see tough times behind you
Maybe there's a blue sky used to be grey
No matter where you go,
you know what it takes to find you
Beneath the weight of all the things that people say

'Cos this person ain't gonna show you
no jive intentions
Ain't gonna sell you no second rate point of view
I been through it all more times
than I care to mention
More times than I ever thought
I could see myself through

You know it's true, You know it's true
That all the things we like to say
Don't speak half as loud as what we do

You know it's true, You know it's true
It's not about the things we say
It's about the things we do

1987

MARC GREGORY

Late Night Lullaby

You have no reason to worry
And nothing to fear
No need for a hurry
When it's perfectly clear

Alone in this place
That you've known for so long
On the odd chance
That you still might belong
On the odd chance
That you still might belong

All of the things
That you thought were you
Fade like winter cold
When a spring rain comes through

And the best things still come
As such a surprise
Like looking in someone
You truly love's eyes
Like looking in someone
You truly love's eyes

Why should it surprise you?
As you come to realise
That everything you thought you knew

Is only a reflection of what it implies
A memento of Soul passing through

You have no reason to worry
And nothing to fear
Why look behind you
When it's all right here
Where there's nothing to fear
When it's perfectly clear
Right here,
Right now

1986

Bottom Line

Why would I mislead you?
Been behind you all along
Always been your own main man
Why would I steer you wrong?

No, what I said was this
Though what you heard was that
And while we're on the subject
It's a bit not where it's at

Something about the image
It isn't just quite right
But I gotta say
The material is tight...
Yeah, pretty tight

But I don't know where to pitch it
Nothing I can do
Maybe a stand in a tribute band
Is something you could do

Bottom line
Bottom line
Bottom line

The line that's on the bottom
does the talking every time

See, we hard-sell on the concept
Wrap it 'round a no-holds clause
When it's all said and done
Who said your soul would end up being yours?

Just keep a step ahead
'Cos who knows what's to come?
Another string of nobodies
Just itching to be a some...

It's like this all over, you know
It just so hard to tell
The good stuff from the garbage
When anything will sell
(Said the label rep from hell...)

Bottom line....

Hear too much of this stuff
Drive you out your goddamned mind
I'd tell him where to pitch it
But God knows what you'd find

When it's style over substance
Zero content is the norm
But used right, all this hyped-up, refried shit
Might keep you warm

Bottom line….

1988

Mind Is Gone*

Mind is gone
Maybe it's just as well
What can I say now?
Words gone wrong
Disordered verse from hell
It's come what may now

Feeble images in my head
Seem to say enough's been said
Still I find it hard to stand
How nothing seems to go as planned
Wine is gone

Ever try
To write a perfect song
And seek words compliant?
Days go by
Still a verse too long
The words are defiant

Failed metaphors scratch and claw
Their pointless way onto your floor
Still, you thought you had something to say
Ideas flicker then blow away
And they're gone

MARC GREGORY

Mind's long gone
Can anybody tell
How very completely
You've gone wrong?
Delusions undispelled
Lose them discreetly

Lines of coffee cups on parade
You've had your share of caffeine today
Try, but you won't understand
The flow of verse running through this man
Mine is gone

2001

*Since first hearing "Year of the Cat" in 1976, I have been a
big fan of Al Stewart, and have followed his career and his
songwriting from their commercial peaks in the late 1970s
through the many excellent, if less well-known albums he has
done since then. This small tribute is written to the tune of a
song of his called "Delia's Gone."*

Got To Have It

Got to have it
Got to have it

It isn't what you're thinking
That really isn't it
Never quite so easy
This cozy little habit

11:37
Too late out of bed
Morning clouds ain't burned off yet
Not around my head

Siren on the nightstand
Soon be screaming straight up noon
So much for sleeping late
Face the long afternoon

Got to have it
What is wrong with me?
Got to have it
Guess it sets me free

Check out the local houses
See who's got the meanest brew
Doesn't mean I'm crazy
Just means more to me than you

Don't go into that one
They let it sit too long
Before they grind another
To keep me hanging on
Hanging on to...

J-J-J-J-Java
Make my problems go away
M-M-M-Mocha Java
Or Nicaraguan anyway
Don't wanna hear no Earl Grey

Don't tell me 'bout Darjeeling
The kick is way too small
Once you have the Big Roast
You got to have it all the time

Fire up Mr. Krups
Throw some cinnamon on top
Nothing like the buzz
To bounce off walls until I drop

I learned all this in Paris
That makes it all okay
It's so sophisticated
When you make it your own way
Your own way with...

J-J-J-J-Java
Gets me through another day
M-M-M-Mocha Java
Or Guatemalan anyway
Don't wanna hear no Earl Grey

I used to really stutter
But now I only shake
I think I'm getting better
Till my head begins to ache
So maybe I'm obsessive
Just a bit uptight
So maybe an espresso
To stay up half the night
Half the night with...

J-J-J-J-Java....

Gorgeous little red-haired girl
Making eyes at me
I hardly even see her
Maybe I should switch to tea

She starts to coming over
What am I gonna do?
My hands are really shaking
Caffeinated through and through
Through and through

Through and through
Through and through with....

J-J-J-J-Java
Make my problems go away....

1985

Any Way You Want Me

Everyone these days is so temperamental
Seems everybody hears a distant call
Map out our lives in gains and potentials
Our conscience sits like a fly upon the wall

We sit and stew over every new step forward
Count all our eggs when there are only some
I wonder what it is that we think we're moving toward
As our hearts, left too long on the run
Wilt like faded postcards in the sun

So in these days of enlightened self-interest
Bust another bonus just for fun
Look down on those who don't measure up to us
Forget about the things we might have done
Is it funny watching others on the run?

Any way you want me
Look hard for what you don't see
Maybe it's too easy
Nothing to it at all

Litigate what might be
Barking up the right tree
I'll take what's in it for me
Any way at all

But now it's time to draw the line
And view it another way
'Cos we are all so very blind
And in such pointless disarray

Everyone these days is so extra-special
Like somehow they're the biggest deal of all
You start to feeling so inconsequential
As if there's some new writing on the wall

All this seems to me so slightly irrational
Like who'll get who to take the biggest fall
Set themselves back up, still so confrontational
Only to not get the point at all
Just to set up someone else to fall

So in these days of stunning indifference
Attitude adjustments just for fun
We seek to find new and better defenses
Just in case somebody jumps the gun
It's plain to see that all of this leads nowhere
That's nowhere to be when your race is run
Nowhere to be when your time is done

Any way you want me
Moving slow does nicely
It's so very easy
Nothing to it at all

Tendering a sweet plea
'Cos the Big Time just set me free
What any fool could see
Any time at all

The things we miss completely
That unfold so discreetly
A view that might set us free
That nothing can forestall

Like taking in a light breeze
Playing through the new leaves
Rustling through the small trees
Waiting for the fall

1990/2009

The Good Witch of the East*

The good witch of the East, it seems
Struggles hard to fit in
Yet refuses to eye a doorway out
Of a world bordering on oblivion

Seeing the feast surrounding others
She strains to remain intact
From a life mapped out by circumstance
Whose wan doldrums their toll exact

Fulfills her role quotidian
Sifts the debris shifting out and in
Hides the scars of deep vermilion
And seeks to hold fast to a truth within

Yet her heart the world would enfold
Labors under burdens long untold
Yearns for a respite from the cold
Well then, who can blame her?
Well then, who can blame her?

Chafes against the ambitious and the brazen
Who slant all truth for personal aim
Self-serving ruses plainly revealing
Unseemly hubris, all humility feigned

Unity a word which some will speak
As if theirs to define and claim
Unity in fracturing what was once whole
Shuffling on others the displaced blame

So an errand here, a meeting there
When something leads to nothing
A barren field, a troubled lair
Aspiring for salvation,
A confirmation of new weather fair
Where nothing leads to something

Hollowed mountains, glimmering prisms
Steel and stone and glass
An ethos of sophomoric neologisms
Adrift before an unseeing mass

And others glitch and fumble still
For pitiable words of self-delivery
Proclaim lame utterances of personal valor
And sound a strange cacophony
Of minds immersed in a collective shallow
And unbecoming vanity

Yet she has a heart of truest gold
Labors under burdens long untold
If she awaits better things to unfold
Well who on Earth can blame her?
Who on Earth can blame her?

The good witch of the East abides
When nothing seems to answer
A path will unfold in time and tide
And she again will be its dancer

2019

For MT with love from her friend MG

What the Heart and Mind Decide

Move through these streets alone
Time after time, after time again
Look back at these things, all loved and known
Without much regard for why and when

Faces come and go, and the good ones too soon
Places and circumstance all start to blend
The impulse comes up, all too quickly consumed
To touch someone I might not see again

These thoughts go rushing by so emphatically
And I try to view them all so impassively
Ah, but somehow it doesn't ride
When I think of how much it all meant to me
These little signs of everything that just might be
What the heart and mind decide

So much comes to mind you thought you'd let go
But a frisson returns that you can't quite explain
A something about a someone you'd know
When the time was just right,
and you could reach out again

All the times you struggled for the right words to say
And you maybe think it didn't matter anyway,
Ah, but it's not easy to be denied
Still you look back, just momentarily

To put some things the way you think they ought to be
How could you ever just let them slide?

When you think you've had enough of the brutality
In a world where nothing's ever as it ought to be
And all you do is let the days roll by
No need to wrestle with each day's eternity
You still might find that there is something to retrieve
Of all the things you left behind
Part of you you hope to find
What the heart and mind decide

Uneven streets without and within
Wondering this time what is to be gained
Sullen impressions of where and when
Shades of reflection never twice the same

1987

Showers

So what will save you
In this desolate hour?
Refracted rainbows dissolve into
Dreary opaque showers

Strewn like dead seaweed
On storm-devoured shore
Helpless to resist waves
Of oceanic power

Showers of words
Showers of tears
Shrouded in tempests
Of imploding fears
And bypassing years

What to do?

Black waves pounding
Upswirling sand
Bits of shoreline reclaimed
By relentless demand

So what will save you
In this dissolute hour
Strewn like dead seaweed
On storm-ravaged shore, devoured?

2001

Song for a Young Girl*

Another again it comes
To an end so hard to take
A young person tragically overcome
An irrevocable mistake

Cashed-in leaders say they seek to protect
Inalienable rights
Empty rhetoric spent to deflect
The price of mean foresight

And as we sit
Watching time go by
This fate will befall others
In the sad blink of an eye

We side-step responsibility
Look to factor blame unknown
Huddle to prevent from complicity
Those dear among our own

But no debate impervious
Can answer for this loss
Ruthless enablers seek bloody profit
At unspeakable cost

What it comes down to—
They are our children
What it amounts to—
They are afraid
No "cornerstone of liberty"
Will voice this truth unsaid

What will we do
To protect them
From this curse that grips us all?
In the silent, aching dread
That no rhetoric can forestall

And as we sit
Watching time go by
This fate remains relentless
Seeking others to crucify
Under the blink of watchless eyes

So I contemplate the better years
She will never see
A future gone, life self-revoked
In tacit misery

And as I watch at gravesite
The horror that can't be undone,
The ineffable grief of a family
That has no place to turn

I curse without reluctance
The path that brings us here,
A nation awash in greed and guns,
Poised and pointed in all manner known,
Reeling in its own corruption,
And choking on its fear

*It is necessary in this country to have a license to drive a car
or a truck, to fly a plane, pilot a boat, practice medicine or
law, sell real estate and so forth. But not to have a gun. The
second amendment to the Constitution addresses the need for
a well-regulated militia in the late 18th century, at a time
when there were no armed forces, nor regular law enforcement
agencies. It has nothing whatsoever to do with indiscriminately
allowing people to arm themselves to the teeth with high-
tech weapons. Nor to make enormous profits from the illicit
merchandising of those weapons. The rest of the civilised world
just shakes its head.*

Life on the Line*

So how many are there
With nowhere to go?
Nothing surrounds them
But the wind blowing cold

Got sunrise at morning
Got sunset at night
Got damn little else
When compassion is slight

You can take it or leave it
Think it's part of a plan
Blank stares on bland faces
Tight cell-fisted hands

But that's just America
Like it or not
Where your value is measured
By the things that you've got
And by appearing
To be what you're not

And it's only a matter of time
When your life is on the line

It's only a matter of time
When your life is on the line

But to some it seems unnatural
Does the heart begin to rend
In a plundered culture shot to hell
Spiraling in its descent?

So you think of the children
Caught in the cold
And the high price they pay
For the values we hold

As if they asked for it
Like it was someplace to be
Like their biggest problem
Wasn't you, wasn't me

But here in America
We just accept it
And we just turn our heads
'Cos we're so full of shit

Fifty stars on blue background
Where we talk a big game

Red stripes sear the have-nots
Leaders white-wash the blame

Because it's convenient
And it's easy and free
When it's all taken care of
And you don't have to be

Part of the many
With nowhere to go
An existence in shadows
Stranded on hold

And it's only a matter of time...

1987/2004

*Homelessness is an embarrassment and a national disgrace. It's
also a problem that could easily enough be solved forever were
we to muster the decency, compassion and political will to do
it. Yet it persists, generally going unacknowledged or ignored
by political leaders of both major parties and all others but
the most progressive. But ignoring problems and pretending
they don't exist doesn't make them go away. It just makes them
worse. And in this case, it holds people in an ignoble captivity
that no-one should have to endure.*

Midwinter Down

Midwinter down
Through a maze of cataclysms
Like thorns in a crown
Ingrained romantic mannerisms

Grey-slated town
Saturated realism
Frozen fields patched with brown
A canvas of internal schism

We both marked in early spring
The passing of the year
A tensile, unexpected rain
Became a vale of tears
Beating down
Sheeting down
As from a tear in a high window sill seam
The rain cues the season's numbing change
The tears the passing of a dream

It takes a long time
To weather all the hidden torrents
Line after line spent to expunge
The inner torment

On and on and on if just to say
The ones that hold our hearts just go away
Each in their own way

Moments that cut the deepest
Forever frozen snapshots in time
Immobile in the closed recesses
Impassive at the base of sharp decline
As shearing ice tears through depth of thawing ground
Trace of long-sown hope cannot be found

Midwinter down
Marks so many hard concessions
The grey-slated town
Fumbles with its misconceptions

It's all turned around
And nothing much matters anymore
So scream without sound
It's all been said and done before

But the dream that passed
Marking not quite another year
Soars home high and free at last
Far beyond the veil of passing years
And well above the vale of flooding tears

2004

Beat to the Wide*

You don't know why you do it
But still you don't see
Another way around
Some reason to believe

Well maybe you found it
And maybe you ain't
As you crawl through the world
Faking the business of saints

Beat to the wide
Hang-dog and fried
Save something inside
Beat to the wide

You hit the ground running
With no place to stop
And your three au laits fail you
As you head for a drop

While down from Montmartre
Drifts a hope second-hand
Through veils of spent canvas
That no dream could withstand

Beat to the wide
From side to side
The pain is implied
Locked up inside

Beat to the wide
Adrift on the tide
Of mass self-delusion
And fuck-ups oft-tried

You used to hear it
Between the two wars
Floating on a gin fizz or three
With certain phantoms
You can still see the scars
Some so deep you wouldn't believe

So make it convincing
But don't give it your all
Tap-dancing the abyss
Of some broken free-fall

Fine a l'eau to unwind you
It may take four or five
Dead leaves in a gutter
You might barely survive

Beat to the wide
From side to side
The struggle's implied
'Cos it's all been tried

Beat to the wide
Save something inside
Something to save you
The last ounce of pride

Beat to the wide
Hang-dog and fried
Gitanes on the sidewalk
Do you feel so alive?

2001

*A song about living in Paris as a young man, some 50 years
after the so-called "Golden Age". "Beat to the wide" was an
idiomatic expression associated with the circle of American and
British expats that included Hemingway and Fitzgerald.

Not Again

Not again
Do I let it slip like cool, clear water
Through my hands
Not again
Watch a fragile balance totter
Not again

You can see it's never-ending
You can just believe it's true
All this lateral condescending
As if they really knew

Once again
A terse solitude enfolds me
Once again
There and then
The short-sighted kind short-sold me
Yet again

Now I sit in this cathedral
Of dispositions all my own
Contemplating primeval
Partitions made of stone

If I willed it all to happen
I guess I never knew
Surrounded by these has-beens
Who never had a clue
Heads of bone, petrified right through

Once again
Angling out of a whirlwind
I wish I had never known...

Now again
Somber recollections
Of days already flown
And possibilities unknown...

1983/2016

The Grifter

"It means 'from God' " it said
As if to upload blame
On long-suffering divinity
A carney's par-boiled claim

"Not to blame, no, not me"
Comes the age-old bastard's cry
From both sides of both faces
Under baggy, averted eyes

"Yeah, that's it, fantastic—
You can help me with my plan"
Make myself rich at your expense
Leave you holding the bag

"Because I care only for justice
For all the human race"
Wouldn't know it slap-shot off a stick,
And pucking in his motherfucking face

See something like this coming
Heed the loathing it instills
Before it sneaks up behind you
Sniffing out its kind of thrills

Like rifling through your wallet
Looking to probe something else
Better look before you sit down
Before it serves itself

Turn away
Lest the urge not be dispelled
The simple impulse, say
To send its fatuous ass to hell

Frame this bust to model
Set a modern master loose
Capture all the obtuse angles
Of this oily Christmas goose

A sharp eye to trace the nuance
Of this jackdaw's wasted life
The boyfriends who'd had enough
The sedated, well-to-do wife

Trails a line of carnage
Says "no, no not to blame"
But this is walking garbage
And by any other name,
By any other name...

2002

Anything You Say

Told you over and over
No point looking back
Head craned over your shoulder
Stuck in your tracks

There's a new world beginning
There's a lot to do
A future for winning
Before you're all through

But day by day
You watch the hours descending
The sidelong frays in sad relief
Parsing shades of grey, you know
You keep befriending
Back-handed voices, collateral grief

So you keep searching the nexus
With your up-cluttered mind
Each scattered fragment still vexes
And the whole's ill-defined

To extract something better
Is like blood from a stone
Latte-fueled whims of chimpanzee financiers
And the bedrock is blown

Anything you say, you know
You're just pretending
With your tattered patchwork of belief
Anymore, it seems
Your position needs defending
Your wagon keeps up-ending
As if in a dream

I don't know where the answer lies, baby
Maybe it's entirely plain
The more you look, the harder to surmise
As the losses surely outweigh the gains
And the same damn emptiness remains

Seek to wake from the nightmare
That martyrs each passing day
Right there in the bright glare
The same old con game prevails

To finesse a transition
To get it all back on track
Ain't no small proposition
With your dignity intact

No matter what the play
You may be intending
The past is gone, the dues sustained
Indulging empty ways
Is the thread, the emblem
Of a pocketful of spent yesterdays

2008

Numbers

Half-dozen eggs gone bad
Back of the third shelf down
Nothing ever makes it out of there
Unless I drop it to the ground

Another 12 calls unanswered
Unavailable by star-69
All of them perched on that 30-day marker
Looking to hang me out to dry

Take your last nickel on a rainy day
Take a shot at your very last dime
And if in all conscience you have nothing to give
Your future looks to get redefined

You can say it's a matter of business
Of not taking in the blind side
But with the scent of blood and salt in the water
The man-eaters are not hard to find

Another jump-start on my '94 Civic
Hanging 225 on the frame
Never thought it would get me half this far
Another rebuild, but it's never the same

22 months of out-of-work checks
Running off my string to 99
22 months since I was downsized
"Rendered redundant", as they said at the time

I worked 30 years to make this house my home
It's the last thing I'll let slip away
My wife and me, we raised our family here
Now she's gone, and they've moved away
Fading sunlight that solitude betrays

And in the evening I sit with the lights out and pray
That what has befallen so many will not pass my way
All the pain
And the stress
The despair
And the mess
Of being broad-brush tarred with other people's sins
Of being at the mercy of some lame Wall Street whim

So much talk about tawdry thoughts
Whose praises the mindless will sing
How can you not look askance
At a fool's dance
Where jokers pretend to be king?

There's only so much blood you can sweat
Till your strength starts to trickle away
And if this is the flow of my ever-after
Siphoning hands look for new places to stray

Into the reaches of other people's pockets
Forcing life after life into disarray
While the LCD work of some bright-spark little clerks
Hovers a haze over each rising day
While the LCD work of some bought-off little jerk
Swelters all like a savannah in May
And the light in the lives of everyday people
Drifts to dusk and fades slowly away

2004

Echoes of Atrocities Past

A long-fated people
Walled in and shut out
Wailing in the streets and fields
Sheets of ear-searing sound

A father draws his toddlers' bodies near
Frantic, a mother clutches her son through her tears
Each immersed in the horror and bitter grace
Of a harrowing, untimely final embrace

Lawn chairs and brews relishing the show
Of projectiles rending the valley below
In a tempest of ghastly wreckage and plunder
The bodies of innocents lie shredded asunder

Echoes of jackboots of another time
Treading a path dark and serpentine
Marching obscenely out of the decay
Of myriad atrocities of a bygone day

Echoes of acts of horror unfurled
Souls condemned to an unholy whirl
Of all that stands where it should not stand
Of every abomination visited upon this land

In the endless slipstream of pillage and plunder
The bodies of innocents now lie piled under
Crushed by the fist of slow-murdering hand
In a world where salvation is but blood in the sand

Contriving an enemy of a people unarmed
Avenging the sound of each false false alarm
Claiming there is something to be now achieved
Sounding echoes of a past in hell conceived
With a reprise of atrocities ever obscene

No verse can capture the revulsion engendered
By those who yet conjure sanity's surrender
They went down before and will not now succeed
Yet usurp every last drop of blood they can bleed.

It will not prevail, nor more will long stand
This nightmare unleashed by unspeakable hand
Now and evermore let its time be run
In the smoldering ruins of atrocities long done.

2017

Now's the Time*

Nothing could be sweeter than to close the deal
Something come to nothing, nothing left to steal
Your job, your home, your life,
you know it's nothing new
Your story's just a lonely gigabyte or two
They call it solid business, just to explain
No matter how they frame it, the result's the same

Fall in line—
You're about to be told what's real
Sleepy time—
Benumbed by the same old schpiel
And if we buy the line on the corporate design
The exit has been sealed

It doesn't really matter if you wonder why
It doesn't really matter just how many cry
World trade culture's a revolving door
Just keep in mind who it's revolving for
The upper tenth of one percent, and that ain't you
The crumbs you hold that trickle down will have to do

Fall in line—
You're about to be told what's real
Sleepy time—
But look who's asleep at the wheel
Smudges 'round the line of the corporate design
There's so much to conceal...
Carnage to conceal

Ah, one and one and one are three
Too many worlds for a planet to hold
In a war-torn corporate destiny
A billion real stories go untold

"Enlightened self-interest" is the buzz of the day
A planet to plunder, so just get out of the way
Not so illuminating being poor
A chewed-up rubber stop on the revolving door
Decades come and go, you know it's still the same
See what you can manage on two bucks a day

Now's the time—
Time to tune in to what's real
Draw the line—
Enough of the same old schpiel
Time to draw the line on the corporate design
And see what stands revealed

Now's the time—
Time to tune in to what's real
We decline—
No more of the bloodstained deals
Time to draw the line on the corporate design
And see what stands revealed

2002

*The bridge in this song obviously riffs on a famous Beatles lyric.
It is no accident that the song paraphrased is "Come Together."
According to yearly reports from Oxfam International, a
small group of the world's richest people have a greater
collective net worth than the entire bottom half of the
world's population, some 3.7 billon people. This imbalance is
historically, practically and morally untenable.*

What's It Gonna Be Today?*

Some people just won't give in
Some people can't put on the brakes
Some people can't learn to put down the fight
No matter how much it takes

Somebody has to stand up
For those who have been left out
For those we've allowed to end up
Where nobody wants to be found

So what's it gonna be today?
And who needs a brow beaten now?
Which silver-tongued, pink-eared,
double-jowled, down-home
champion of freedom
Won't bring himself to see how?

Something like this could be important
That your ideas are not a mistake
That a path diverting from his one-track agenda
Might be a path to take

And some even said you were crazy
Because you tried to explain
That when you're down, and your luck has run out
Down is where you might remain
To spend the rest of your numbered days

And it's always the same old story
When you have to shout and shout to be heard
By teary-eyed morons who've made public careers
Out of not keeping their word
To the people they're elected to serve

So what's it gonna be today?
What's it gonna be today?
Who's gonna have nothing but
the same old shit to say?
What's it gonna be today?

'Cos now we're up to our asses in the shattered glass
Of broken lives that didn't mend
Cashed in against a future they never had in this land
That we've paid through the nose to defend

This land of big, broken promises
And of dreams that didn't come true
Where the end is justified by just any means
Well there's only so much you can do
Yeah, there's only so much you can do

So it came as a shock as these things always do
Guess it was only a matter of time
You give out and give out,
until something in you gives out
And no more reason can you seem to find
Not to leave the struggle behind

1991

*Written, with humility, as a loose tribute to homeless advocate
Mitch Snyder, who died in 1990.*

But They Were Mine

It was four years ago December
One small room wasn't enough
I don't know if they'll remember
But for me, it's all I can think of

And in the intervening silence
Has passed so much wasted time
As I curse the stifling compliance
To which I must be resigned

They told me it was all for the best
As if it wasn't easy to say
When life should have held for you better things
Than just enduring day to day
In circumstantial decay

It wasn't right, it wasn't fair
To deprive them of the chance
I never could provide them
That passed me by without a glance
Without even a backwards glance

But they were mine
Doesn't matter how many years

One look and time
Unravels in tatters
The past never quite so near

It killed me when they took them then
And it hurts like hell to this day
To be told by total strangers
That I'll have nothing to say

Or to do but to let them go
With no trace in their hearts and minds
As I take up this race I can never win
To begin a again a life misplaced
By so much long-lost time

It was four years ago December
Maybe someday they'll understand
The reason it's hard to remember
The empty fate that forced my hand

And on this frozen winter night
My blessings number but one
Though I can see in, no-one can see out
And this illusion can't be undone
A homeless tale long since spun

But they were mine
And nothing can ever change that
Though after all these years
It might somehow how seem strange
That I'd remember time and distance only go so far
They were once mine
And they still are

1993

The Greatest Country in the World

Seniors rifling through recycling
For an extra nickel or a dime
Like somehow it's a privilege to do it
When you're well past sixty-five

Young people saddled with crushing debt
Can't count the countless homeless vets
For these there is no safety net
Here in the greatest country in the world.

Leverage a lifetime for a doctor's care
When it all goes on the line
Unravelling in the press of the wear and tear
The edge of the precipice is too fine

Working three jobs to scratch out a life
Trying to manage the internal strife
And the tension cuts like a dull-edged knife
All in the greatest country in the world

High-tech thugs dog people of color
And laugh in pursuit of the destitute
Subverting the law that grants their order
Immune to any countersuit

Billions spent on armaments
Crowded cities, bleak tenements
Glorified closets, sky-high rents
Social isolation, then a skid-row tent
All in the greatest country in the world.

Some of us saw it rising
Steadily grew the fleurs du mal
Pushed aside in the compromising
And distraction hovers like a pall
In the endless lie that hides it all

Misinfo from brainless talking heads
Stoking constant fear and dread
Looking for any truth they can shred
All in the greatest country in the world

There was a time when gentler winds blew
Not for all, of course, but for some
Amid the descent of this harsh curfew
Tired souls are made cold and numb

By the smug and self-important
Those crashing seats at the table
Shielded with ill-gotten fortune
Stealing everything they're able

Brutalized minorities
Separated families
Blighted inner cities
All in the daily by and by

Boldly-voiced hypocrisies
Oft-repeated insanities
Long-misplaced humanity
All in the daily do or die

Some are trying to save it
To offset the estrangement
To dial down how depraved it has become

Time to hit the pavement
To protest the enslavement
Until this craven nightmare's day is done

What can you say of a people
Who abandon their own children
Letting them linger in anguish
In a macabre charade, bewildered?

What can you say of a people
Who choose the vile to lead them,
Grant power to the irredeemable,
And persecute those who would free them?

You say awakening is painfully slow
You wait for some awareness to grow
You deplore the grotesque ebb and flow
In the greatest country in the world
All in the greatest country in the world
All in the greatest country in the world….

2019

Never

Never did I think that I would fall this way again
Never did I think that I could wall away the pain
And keep it out
And leave it there
And hear it shout
Well that ain't fair

Careening through old memories always raises a sigh
A bland excuse emblazoned in a past adorned
with whys
Just let them go
And let them fly
Just tell them no
And let them die

Eyes downcast, all you ever see is the same old thing
Iconoclast, alone, immune to what the day may bring

Whether this will last or not I really cannot say
If it will see me all the way home, for that I pray
Without a doubt
Nothing unclear
Leave the last bout
Without a fear

Clever is the man who can think and do and say
Ever all in a straight line each and every day
And make it last
And keep it whole
Until the last
As years unfold

2013

Not So Long Ago

Not so long ago
It was easy to remember
That the only thing that mattered
Was how you played the game
Along the way

Not so long ago
Circumstances neatly gathered
To force me to realise
All the things I knew
And couldn't say

Everything in time
About softly windswept changes
And gentle re-arranges
Of all the things you used to be

Seems to happen by design
Everything you ask for
And sometimes even much more
Much more than all the things
You do or say

But years go rushing by
And so many dreams get shattered

Sift the remnants of how and why
Still you don't seem to break the pattern
Of countless hours in stillborn days

Every mistake you made
Carves its own path back to haunt you
Deals its own rough trade
In all the things you never wanted
And all the things that passed you by

Every now and then
As in a softly gathered leaf-fall
Moments passed compress in recall
Fragments of time together
You and me

But now I guess they're gone
Like a high wind through the desert
Moving dust across the seasons
Swirling down to die where none can see

Not so long ago
Circumstances neatly gathered
To force me to recognise
All the things I knew and couldn't say

Not so long ago
It was easy to remember

That the only thing that mattered
Was how you played the game along the way
How you played the game along the way
How you played the game along the way...

Not so long ago

1988

As it Came to Pass (A Certain Time of Day)

I grew up in the sixties
In a quiet little corner of L.A.
Brown skies left over from the decade before
But there was always a safe place to play

Working-class kids from working-class families
Looking to move up along the way
Some of them did, some of them didn't
We never knew it mattered either way

Shield my eyes, peel away the years
Look through the shabby mirage of today
There beneath decades of idle change
Shimmerings of another time remain

Summer cloudburst-slick top-dust on asphalt
Comes a strong gust to blow the storm away
Breathe in the rain-cooled clear in the air
See what's left of a new sunny day

The rustling fever of crickets in June
August sweltering as midnight slips away
A neighborhood glued to the banter on Carson
The heat breaks on a small breeze
At the end of a mid-summer day

Just working class, as it came to pass
Rising out of a common post-war past
Where you did what you had to just because
You couldn't know what the coming reality was

Under wind-drawn skies in the early fall
Leaves that crackle underfoot and blow away
The sun traced the shape of the shade
in your front yard
Always at a certain time of day

California dreaming*
Past to the present
The last shade of childhood
Burning off in adolescence

Retroactive scheming
Present to the past
Looking for the shelter of
Something inside you that lasts

Cloudbreak rolls north through the canyons
Minutes pass like hours at the end of school
Butterfly handlebars, daredevil abandon
And made to be broken are all rules
When you're ten years old and just out of school
When you're ten years old and nobody's fool

Nothing lasts as it came to pass
Never thought twice about looking back
From a future where it'd be safe to say
Nothing could have ever gone astray
But was anything ever safe to say?

The mirage returns, the decades recede
The new breed think they're way too chic to say
But beneath the glare of easy nouveau money
Seasons of another time sustained

With the dance of sunlight off windows in the hills
And the soft elms that are always there to stay
Tracing the shape of years stretching before you
And all that was always on its way

Distant childhood voices are never stilled
Like leaves in November, they just go their way
Traces of it all, like the wind-drawn skies in the
early fall
Softly abide to this day
And the shade of the elms falling gently inside you
Is forever locked safely away

1993

*John Phillips' and The Mamas and Papas' "California Dreamin'"
is one of the definitive songs of its era, and a song indelibly
woven into my childhood and early adolescence.*

Early Fallen for Summer

Soft mid-afternoon light
Savoured reflections
Of everything you thought would always be
One by one they turn and fade
Adrift in phosphorescent shade
And flicker off into eternity

A "did-it-have-to-happen?"
Prompts a diffident murmur
As those who seem to know seek to explain
Words are spent in frail discourse
That strays to convey a contained remorse
Collapsing phrases trapped in dull refrain

And yet it should be simple
To get across the meaning
Of time and life and loss and too much pain
And a somber ever-after
That shimmers and ripples
A relentless wind through fields of heat-singed grain

Strange late-afternoon light
Early fallen for summer

That dances on a slow-unfolding breeze
Hopes and dreams now all undone
Rage into that oblivion
That rolls beneath the tide of endless seas

2006

Calendar of Moons

Moving like a whisper in a distant foreign land
Through dragon's breath and tumbling hoops of fire
Ashes of a forgotten dream
Smolder overhead
And flutter in the air above a pyre
    Of memories
    Misapprehensions
    Missed cues
    Misconstrued intentions

Looking over the ocean
That stretches on forever
From the rocky outcrop mountains coastal to this land
White caps on the winter sea
Glimmer then expire
Crests of foam dissolve upon the sand
    Thoughts rise
    Then vaporise
    The sea recedes
    Absorbing grey skies

I will not play the fool
For an indiscriminate creature
And dance upon an unraveling high wire
I will not watch the days fall
Nor re-negotiate my cool
Ambling through the dregs of misplaced desire

I speak to those around me
With eyes and heart and hands
And the simple words I can remember
Despite my wayward phrases
They seem to understand
The spirit of my meaning as it's rendered

And life is lived as it is lived here
On a calendar of moons
As the sun shoots through the panes of high-rise spires
Buffeted by motion
An all-enveloping cocoon
I step away from the entangling wire
     Of failed hopes
     Misconceptions
     Missed mystical cues
     Misapplied contentions

Some bring misery inescapable
Some the hint of treasure unforeseen
But you'll forever remain replaceable
To pre-disposed hearts it seems,
Like the wisp of a forgotten dream

Rolling like a cloudbank
In a far-off distant land
Through laughing grace and sprays of tumbling fire
Some things, as it happens, I will never understand
I turn away from an all-consuming mire
And the vanity to which I long ago aspired

2013

Look Ahead

Wintry footsteps on soggy ground
Leaf clusters scattered in the rain
The scent of rust on the freezing breeze
December arrives with a sheet-metal strain

Grey down the coast as gales stir
Bar Harbor to the Carolinas
The swarming thoughts of twenty-odd years
Jagged shards, a million harsh reminders

Glass and metal are the frames
Of this internal landscape
Blowing off your heat shields
With each invernal scrape
Brittle figures gesture wildly
Grotesquely pirouetting
Breathlessly I lose my stride
With all this internal misbegetting
Ah the power of regretting...

Look ahead
Now there's nothing behind for you
It's all been done and said
So look up in time for you

Nothing more to dread
Let this somehow remind you to
Make it shine instead...

Shuttle back through faceless years
Turning in circles, arriving nowhere
Looking in corners of elliptical rooms
For a hint or a clue how to get there

There is a place that never was
A dream between time and eternity
Where things that will be and never were collide
In the shadows of things that we don't see

Look ahead...
Now there's nothing unkind for you
It's all been done and said
So look up in time for you

Nothing more to dread
Let this somehow remind you to
Make it shine instead
And see what you find in you
And see what's in line for you
And live unconfined in you...

Take a day, take a year
Take a lifetime to make it clear
Take a pass, take a powder
Take a fader and make it louder

Now I'm talking about zero strain
Laughingly caught in a summer rain
A morning breeze embrace
And a pocket charm just in case...

Look ahead...

2014

Nothing Left to Say

Writing for the fun
Of drawing a pen across some paper
Something comes to mind
Nothing comes to mind
And all my living hard
Didn't make it easier

Pick up the receiver
Ring the number I know so well
There's someone on the line
Another voice, not mine
Someone new, you can never tell
What the hell—
If you could only tell

Nothing left to say
So I say it the complicated way
With all sorts of wordplay
It gets so complicated to
Say just what you mean
Talk of things that might have been
But for now remain unseen

Nothing left to say
Though I thought we had forever

MARC GREGORY

We wore so many faces
Put our hearts in different places
And all our living hard didn't make it easier
Now all this dying hard doesn't make it easier
When there's nothing left to say

1986

www.ingramcontent.com/pod-product-compliance
Lightning Source LLC
LaVergne TN
LVHW011202080426
835508LV00007B/550